Versailles: The History and Legacy of France's

By Charles River Edito

A Toucan Wings aerial drone photo of Versailles

About Charles River Editors

Charles River Editors is a boutique digital publishing company, specializing in bringing history back to life with educational and engaging books on a wide range of topics. Keep up to date with our new and free offerings with this 5 second sign up on our weekly mailing list, and visit Our Kindle Author Page to see other recently published Kindle titles.

We make these books for you and always want to know our readers' opinions, so we encourage you to leave reviews and look forward to publishing new and exciting titles each week.

Introduction

Versailles

"Growing up in Versailles is like growing up in a museum, and the people living there are almost the security." – Thomas Mars

In every nation, in every era of history, there are inevitably one or two places that become the symbol of the times. Mention Valley Forge to an American and it will immediately conjure up visions of a hard won fight for freedom. Likewise, the word Dunkirk said to a Briton will elicit a sense of both pride and horror at the lives lost and saved at that desperate point in World War II. For the French, and those who study their history, Versailles is a symbol of, as Charles Dickens once put it, "the best of times…the worst of times." It was here that the Sun King, Louis XIV, built a palace worthy of a great nation during a time when peace was, at best, short-lived. It was at Versailles that Russian Tsar Peter the Great to study the palace's architecture and gardens so that he could recreate them in his home country. Indeed, the greatest minds and artistic geniuses of the later stages of the Renaissance came to Versailles to build and paint, and it was here that Madame de Pompedour and her successor, Madame du Barry, used their wit and beauty to charm a king into doing their bidding.

However, as history constantly demonstrates, nothing good lasts forever, and so it was with Versailles. From the royal palace, Louis XVI and Queen Marie Antoinette frittered away the goodwill of their people, leading to the French Revolution and their executions. Here the mobs amassed to demand "freedom, equality and brotherhood," but mainly a piece or two of pilfered bric-a-brac. In the wake of the French Revolution, the palace was gutted and most of the beautiful reminders of its glory were sold away, along with the monarchy's birthright and the concept of the "divine right of kings."

While the palace was neglected for a time, its original workmen had done their jobs well enough that it managed to weather both time and the political storms that raged around it during the early 19th Century. In fact, it seems as though Versailles was destined to survive, if only so that such a thing of beauty wouldn't be lost forever. Even as he focused on the rest of Europe, Napoleon felt the need to save Versailles, and over time it was restored to its original glory, if not its original purpose; no monarch has lived in Versailles for a long time. Instead, there is a republic, and with it a sense that the palace, once available only for the wealthy few, is now a place for people across the world to come and enjoy the splendor of a bygone era that, while not exactly missed, can nonetheless still be appreciated.

Versailles: The History and Legacy of France's Most Famous Royal Palace chronicles the remarkable history of one of the world's most famous palaces and tourist spots. Along with pictures depicting important people, places, and events, you will learn about Versailles like never before.

Versailles: The History and Legacy of France's Most Famous Royal Palace
About Charles River Editors
Introduction
   King Louis XIV and the Origins of Versailles
   Enlarging Versailles
   Life at Versailles
   The Influence of Versailles
   Online Resources
   Further Reading
Free Books by Charles River Editors
Discounted Books by Charles River Editors

King Louis XIV and the Origins of Versailles

The earliest record for any place called Versailles dates back to the Charter of Saint-Pere de Chartres Abbey from 1038. One of the men signing this document called himself Hugo de Versailles, the seigneur (Lord). At this time, Versailles was little more than a village that had grown up around the small castle that Hugo had built for his family to live in. There was also a church under his patronage, where he and those he was responsible for could regularly receive the sacraments. These two buildings were located on the road between Paris and Normandy, so there was enough foot traffic for a few merchants to ply their trade. However, many of those living in the area died of plague, and many of the men who survived lost their lives in the Hundred Years War. Thus, the village stood largely empty for years. It was not until 1575 that Albert de Gondi, who had come to France from Florence, Italy and had gained favor with Henry II, was able to purchase the castle and the surrounding village, as well as the title of Seigneur of Versailles.

Albert de Gondi

Very little of interest happened at Versailles until the reign of Louis XIII, when Gondi invited the new king to come to Versailles to visit and hunt. The forests were teeming with birds and deer, and the king enjoyed himself immensely, so much so that he had a hunting lodge built there in 1624 for his personal use. According to early 20th Century historian Francis Loring Payne, "Louis' architect was Philbert Le Roy, and the new villa was about two hundred feet from the lodge first constructed. Its form was a complete square, each corner being terminated by a tower. The building was of brick, ornamented with columns and gilded balustrades; it was surrounded by a park adorned with statues sculptured after designs by the artist Poussin. Ambitious addition!" However, Payne noted that not everyone was impressed: "The court resented the enterprise, the nobility despised it. It was the King's fancy; nothing else excused it. A noble of the court, Bassompierre, exclaimed that 'it was a wretched château in the construction of which no private gentleman could be vain.'"

Louis XIII

Louis hunted contentedly from his chateau for eight years before he decided he needed more. On April 8, 1632, the king began to expand his hunting lodge into a larger, more comfortable living space, and he continued working on the house until he died in 1643, at which time the area fell into disrepair and many of the nobles who had built cottages around it moved back to larger homes in and around Paris.

When Louis was on his deathbed in May 1643, he had the 4 year old Dauphin brought to him. Upon asking the young child if he knew who he was, the Dauphin replied, "Louis the Fourteenth, Father." His father rebuked the boy, telling him, "You are not Louis the Fourteenth yet." A few days later, Louis XIII was dead, and at 4 years and 8 months old, Louis XIV became King of France.

Louis XIII had succeeded his assassinated father as a child and came of age with a regent council controlling power until he was in his late teens. Thus, in his will he tried to establish a similar model for his young son. Upon his death, however, Queen Anne of Austria had his will annulled, which had the effect of doing away with a regent council, thereby making her the sole regent. Even still, young Louis XIV had a happier childhood than many royal children. Following his father's death, his close relationship with his mother continued, even as she effectively ruled. Anne took a strong interest in his education and upbringing, ensuring Louis was provided an academic education, a religious one, a social one and a physical one. The young King was well-read, taught to be pious and devout, and socially cultured. He was also encouraged to ride, hunt and swim.

Anne with the future King Louis XIV of France, and Philippe I, Duke of Orléans

While Louis had held the right to political power since his 13th birthday, his coronation took place on June 7, 1654. The grand affair lasted for hours at the Cathedral of Rheims, the traditional choice for the crowning of a French king, with Anne of Austria watching from a box at the sidelines. Though Anne retained a great deal of power within the court and over her son, that power began to gradually fade as the king grew older and bolder. The young king was well-regarded by his court for his grace, beauty, and dignity, and his royal stature and composure was considered remarkable for his age.

A portrait of young Louis XIV

It would be several years before Louis XIV went out hunting on his father's land near Versailles and discovered the same passion for the area. The house he found was opulent by modern middle-class standards but nothing special for a Renaissance king. The main entrance was flanked on either side by two wings, and there was a screen across the entrance court to provide some privacy. Each of the four corners of the building had a tower, and the entire structure was surrounded by a moat. There were also two service wings that bordered a forecourt set off by two round towers. In 1660, Louis brought his new bride, Maria Theresa, to stay at the lodge, and after that visit the two decided to expand it into a palace fit for their needs and those of their future children.

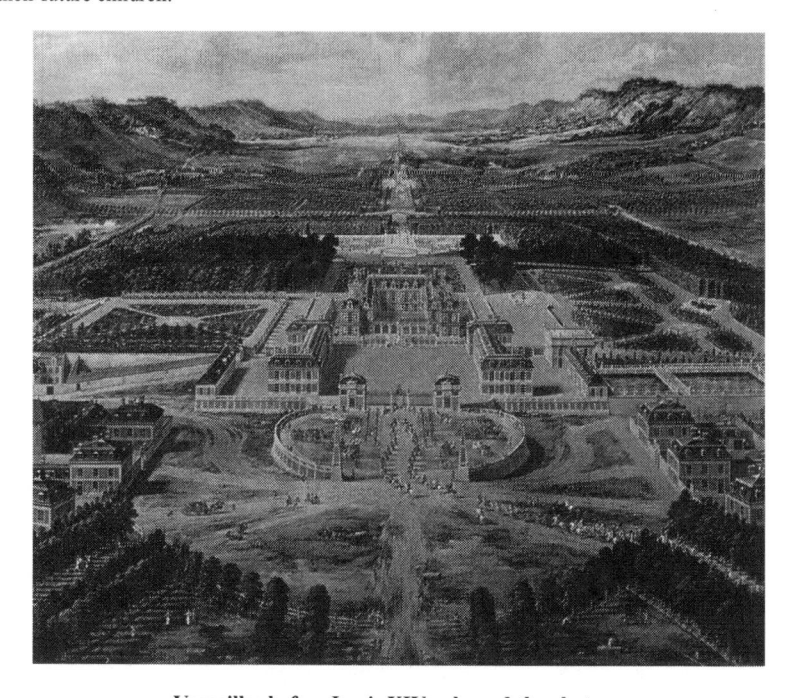

Versailles before Louis XIV enlarged the chateau

Maria Theresa

Louis XIV is best remembered for the grand palace of Versailles, which exceeded all other structures in France in its expense and grandeur, but Versailles was not Louis' first building project. Early in his reign, Louis began working with an architect who would define the style of his time, Louis Le Vau. Le Vau had built pavilions for the King and Queen in Vincennes, worked on the Louvre, and made modifications to the Tuileries. He also worked for parliamentarians and others in Paris, building grand townhouses, including Vaux-Le-Vicomte. Vaux-Le-Vicomte, built for the financier Nicolas Fouquet, was certainly the grandest construction ever completed outside of the royal family. Other artists and architects hired by Fouquet also came to work on Versailles. Le Vau's style was influenced by Italian architecture, favoring classical shapes with baroque detailing.

Vaux-Le-Vicomte

Enlarging Versailles

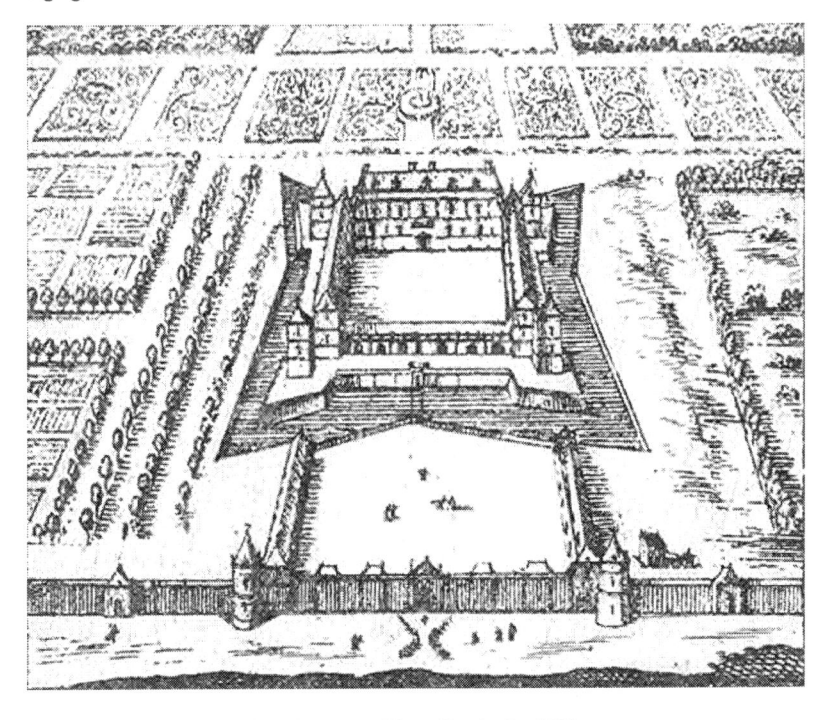

The chateau at Versailles in the 1630s

    The moment Louis made plans to start building at Versailles, officials around him advised against it. Architects suggested that he pursue an alternate course of action, and his Superintendent of Finances, Jean-Baptiste Colbert, opposed his plans, insisting in a letter, "Your majesty knows that, apart from brilliant actions in war, nothing marks better the grandeur and genius of princes than their buildings, and that posterity measures them by the standard of the superb edifices that they erect during their lives. Oh, what a pity that the greatest king, and the most virtuous, should be measured by the standard of Versailles! And there is always this misfortune to fear."

Colbert

Despite the opposition, Louis pursued his plans nonetheless. In 1661, modest improvements to the grounds began, including gardens designed by André Le Nôtre and an orangerie or orange tree grove and menagerie designed by Louis Le Vau. André Le Nôtre's garden plans created a series of elegant outdoor rooms with sculpture, plantings and water features.

Even as Louis kept building, Colbert kept complaining that the king was spending too much money, that he should pay more attention to the Louvre Palace, and that the people were growing restless with the new taxes. In the end, however, the Sun King got what he wanted, and in short order, Versailles grew into one of the largest and most elegant palaces in the world.

Three men helped Louis achieve his goal. The first was Louis Le Vau, the architect who designed much of the building. André Le Nôtre was the landscape architect in charge of designing and developing the gardens, while Charles Le Brun painted the interiors, including many of the magnificent murals that still grace its halls. All three had previously worked for Nicolas Fouquet, the former finance minister, building his great home at Vaux-le-Vicomte. Perhaps jealous of his minister's successful housing project, Louis announced that Fouquet must have embezzled money from his to finance it. In 1661, he confiscated the estate and its three designers.

Louis Le Vau

André Le Nôtre

Charles Le Brun

Fouquet

For Louis, and later for others in the nation, the palace became a symbol of much more than just beauty; it was also a symbol of Louis' spreading power, for as the palace grew, so did his ego. The first hint of what was to come came in 1661 when Cardinal Mazarin died. He had been the king's chief minister of government for years, and when he was gone, Louis announced that he would not replace him but instead act as his own chief minister. He also began to slowly move his court to Versailles, where he felt he would have more control over his advisors.

Since even the French king had limited resources and was often distracted with affairs of state, Louis ended up working on Versailles in five separate phases. It is charming to note that one of the first areas that Louis completed inside the palace was an apartment for his new son, born in November 1661. He also enlarged the house and gardens slightly between 1662 and 1663. The king seemed to be omnipresent during this time.

Payne described some of these initial modifications: "The original entrance court was greatly enlarged. Long wings terminated by pavilions bordered it. On the right were the kitchens, with quarters for the domestics; on the left, the stables, where there were stalls for fifty-four horses. At the main entrance to the court were pavilions used by the musketeers as guard-houses...On the site of the park a great terrace was bordered by a parterre in the shape of a half-moon, where a waterfall was later installed. A long promenade, now called the Allée Royale, extended to a vast basin named the Lake of Apollo. Streamlets were diverted to feed fountains. Twelve hundred and fifty orange trees were transported from the fallen estate of Vaux to fill the long arcades of the orangery."

Meanwhile, Colbert recorded that the Crown spent in excess of 1,500,000 pounds on the renovations in those first few years, but he had to concede in September 1663 that the gold and silver filigree work executed in the Asian style was exquisite: "Never had China itself seen so many examples of this work together--nor had all Italy seen so many flowers." Another writer during this period wrote, "Although, it has not the great size that is to be remarked in some of His Majesty's other Palaces, it is charming in every respect, everything smiles within and without, gold and marble vie with one another in their beauty and brilliancy.... Its symmetry, the richness of its furniture, the beauty of its walks and the infinite number of its flowers and orange-trees, render the surroundings of this spot worthy of its own remarkable beauty."

The next phase, the first major push for renovations, lasted from 1664, when Louis became serious about the project and turned his full attention to it, to 1668, when he had to set aside his improvements in order to fight a war with Spain.

Louis kicked off this phase with a huge fete known as the Plaisirs de l'Île enchantée ("The Pleasures of the Enchanted Island"). Held from May 7-13, 1664, Louis claimed it was in honor of his mother and his wife, but those in the know realized that he was actually honoring his mistress, Louise de La Valliere. In fact, some believe that it was his affection for La Valliere that drove him to Versailles in the first place. The Duc de Saint-Simon, a courtier, wrote, "His love-affair with Mademoiselle de la Vallière, which at first was covered as far as possible with a veil of mystery, was the cause of frequent excursions to Versailles. This was at that time at small country house, built by Louis XIII to avoid the unpleasant necessity, which had sometimes befallen him, of sleeping at a wretched wayside tavern or in a windmill, when benighted out hunting in the forest of St. Leger...The visits of Louis XIV becoming more frequent, he enlarged the château by degrees till its immense buildings afforded better accommodation for the Court than was to be found at St. Germain, where most of the courtiers had to put up with uncomfortable lodgings in the town. The Court was therefore removed to Versailles in 1682, not long before the Queen's death. The new building contained an infinite number of rooms for courtiers, and the King liked the grant of these rooms to be regarded as a coveted privilege...He loved splendour, magnificence, and profusion in all things, and encouraged similar tastes in his Court; to spend money freely on equipages and buildings, on feasting and at cards.... Motives of policy had something to do with this; by making expensive habits the fashion, and, for people in a certain position, a necessity, he compelled his courtiers to live beyond their income, and gradually reduced them to depend on his bounty for the means of subsistence. ...a man of any position is now estimated entirely according to his expenditure on his table and other luxuries."

Plays, ballets, equestrian events, and a lottery with grand and lavish prizes all marked the start of a tradition of lavish parties and festivals at Versailles. While the festival and celebrations surrounding The Pleasures of the Enchanted Island were impressive, they were small compared to what would follow, largely due to the size of the chateau.

Much of the fete took place in the Royal Walk, where the "great path that is at the end of the parterre leads to a very spacious circle, which is traversed by another path of the same width. This spot, which is five or six hundred paces from the Palace, was chosen as the most suitable for the display of the first entertainments in Alcina's enchanted palace."

In the years that followed, Louis had the palace expanded to house the people he wished to entertain, sometimes as many as 600 at a time. He also had smaller dwellings where his favorites could live built on the property. This sent yet another message to the members of his court that change was afoot, and rumors began to spread that Louis intended to make Versailles his permanent and official home. Either way, it was clear he intended it to be a very comfortable community, and he even ordered the construction of an elegant zoo containing "the most splendid palace of animals in the world." He saw to their installation and care himself, and then scattered sculptures of various animals, as well as their mythological counterparts, around the palace.

Louis was nearly finished with his great project, or at least his subjects hoped he was, when his work was interrupted by the War of Devolution in 1667 and 1668. This conflict involved France's attempt to push Spain out of the Spanish Netherlands and the area of Burgundy, but the Sun King's desire for conquest was thwarted by the combined forces of England, Sweden, and the Dutch Republic.

However, as soon as the Treaty of Aix-la-Chapelle was signed and the war brought to an end, he was right back to work on his favorite project. In 1668, before Le Vau's grand changes to the chateau, Louis XIV held another great entertainment, although this one was limited to a single day. It was, nonetheless, an expensive day, called the Grande Divertissement. The gardens were not complete, but courtiers enjoyed a lavish day of plays and feasting in the surprisingly mature garden. Rather than waiting for trees to grow, Louis XIV ordered mature trees brought to Versailles.

In the meantime, the delay had given Le Vau two years to think of improvements, and he was ready to get back to work in 1668. In fact, he had decided that he could make the palace even more spectacular than previously imagined. He showed the king plans that involved tearing down buildings already begun and replacing them with bigger and more opulent structures. However, Louis wanted to retain the original chateau for sentimental reasons, forcing Le Vau to return with a plan for a larger palace to envelop or encompass the original chateau in 1668. The increase in size was essential, because the king was spending more and more time at Versailles and wished to move the government to the "country" palace. The envelop design also included pavilions for the ministers, making it easy for Louis to govern. This would surround the chateau on three sides, providing a new facade and a more stylish flat roof. The enlargement of the chateau, placed on a hill, required significant engineering, including massive terraces, and some 40,000 workers were required to build the envelope, working day and night. The Sun King asked the Church to allow the workers to continue working even on feast days, and the work was extremely dangerous, resulting in many deaths. While Louis originally planned to complete the process by eventually restyling the original chateau, Versailles still essentially remains a palace-within-a-palace.

A contemporary depiction of the construction at Versailles in 1669

Louis also expanded the size of the village around that castle, for if he was going to move his court to the area, the vast number of servants, courtiers, and other hangers on would also need places to live. Around the same time, he charged Le Nôtre with expanding the gardens. One contemporary writer recalled that "when Le Nôtre had traced out his ideas, he brought Louis XIV to the spot to judge the distribution of the principal parts of their ornamentation. He began with two grand basins which are on the terrace in front of the chateau, with their magnificent decorations. He explained next his idea of the double flight of stairs, which is opposite the center of the palace, adorned with yew-trees and with statues, and gave in detail all the pieces that were to enrich the space that it included. He passed then to the 'Allée du Tapis Vert,' and to that grand place where we see the head of the canal, of which he described the size and shape, and at the extremities of whose arms he placed the Trianon and the Menagerie."

No 17th century garden would be complete without a maze, and one writer from Amsterdam described the one at Versailles in 1682: "Amongst all these works there is nothing more admirable and praiseworthy than the Royal Garden at Versailles, and, in it, the Labyrinth. Other representations are commonly esteemed because they please the eye, but this because it not only delights the ear and eye, but also instructs and edifies…This Labyrinth is situated in a wood so pleasant that Daedalus himself would have stood amazed to behold it. The Turnings and Windings, edged on both sides with green cropt hedges, are not at all tedious, by reason that at every hand there are figures and water-works representing the mysterious and instructive fables of Aesop, with an explanation of what Fable each Fountain representeth carved on each in black marble. Among all the Groves in the Park at Versailles the Labyrinth is the most to be recommended, as well for the novelty of the design as the number and diversity of the fountains that with ingenuity and 'naïveté' express the philosophies, of the sage Aesop…The animals of colored bronze are so modeled that they seem truly to be in action. And the streams of water that come from their mouths may be imagined as bearing the words of the fable they represent. There are a great number of fountains, forty in all, each different in subject, and of a style of decoration that blends with the surrounding verdure. At the entrance to the Maze is a bronze statue of Aesop himself--the famous Mythologist of Phrygia."

Le Nôtre may have been a genius at landscaping, but apparently he made for a poor diplomat. According to the same writer, "At each of the grand pieces whose position Le Nôtre marked, and whose future beauties he described, Louis XIV interrupted him, saying, 'Le Nôtre, I give you twenty thousand francs.' This magnificent approbation was so frequently repeated that it annoyed Le Nôtre, whose soul was as noble and disinterested as that of his master was generous. At the fourth interruption he stopped, and said brusquely to the King, 'Sire, Your Majesty shall hear no more. I shall ruin you.'"

A 1674 engraving depicting the garden front

A depiction of the garden facade

Wandernder Weltreisender's picture of one of Versailles' fountains

There is a saying in advertising that sex sells, and when it came to Versailles, it compelled Louis to do more building. In 1670, he ordered a low-lying area called the Marais constructed next to the Fountain of Latona, primarily to please his mistress at the time, Madame de Montespan. While she remained in favor, one chronicler reported that "people spoke of the 'Marais' as one of the marvels of the gardens, but it was undoubtedly considered less wonderful after her fall…In the center stood a large oak surrounded by an artificial marsh, bordered with reeds and grasses, and containing plants and a number of white swans. From the swans, from the reeds and grasses, and from the leaves and branches of the oak, thousands of little jets of water leaped forth, falling like fine rain upon the masses of natural vegetation that flourished amid the artificial. At the sides of the bosquet there were two tables of marble, on which a collation was served when the marquise came to her grove to see the waters play…In 1704 the King ordered Mansard to destroy the 'Marais' and transform the bosquet into the Baths of Apollo."

When the original enveloping design was largely completed, Louis moved his government to Versailles, and the ministers of the Royal Council also moved into Versailles. While Louis lived and governed from Versailles, the nobles and court would not reside there until 1682, when

Louis ordered the entire court to Versailles. In addition to turning Versailles into the ultimate center of power, requiring the nobility to live at Versailles allowed Louis XIV to watch closely over the nobles, reducing the risk of uprisings.

Of course, moving the entire court there would require yet more enlargements to the Palace of Versailles. Le Vau did not live to see his great project completed (he died in 1670), but Jules Hardouin-Mansart took over the construction of Versailles and ably designed large wings for each side of the palace. These large wings would provide housing for the nobility. Unlike most palaces, the wings at Versailles extend toward the back, creating a wide open front court for the gardens and helping to hide the original 16th century construction.

Hardouin-Mansart

The interior court at Versailles

In 1674, official court historian André Félibien wrote of Versailles, "One can say of Versailles that it is a place where Art works on its own, and which Nature seems to have abandoned in order to allow the king, by performing, if I may say so, an act of creation, to bring forth numerous magnificent works and an infinite number of extraordinary things. And in the entire royal house there is no place where Art had [succeeded] more felicitously than in the Grotto of Thetis." That same year, the king authorized an official description of the palace to be printed. Its author gushed, "As the Sun is the device of the King, and poets represent the Sun and Apollo as one, nothing exists in this superb dwelling that does not bear relation to the Sun divinity."

Félibien

Water always played a major role in the Versailles, from the shooting fountains in the gardens to the flowing hot and cold water in the bathroom. In 1675, Louis ordered the famous Three Fountains built. Located between the Avenue of Waters and the château, they were, according to one farmer, "an immense number of small jets of water, leaping from basins at the sides and forming an arch of water overhead, beneath which one could walk without being wet…The Arch of Triumph filled the end of the bosquet; it was placed on an estrade with marble steps, and was preceded by four lofty obelisks of gilded iron in which the water leaped and fell in sheets of crystal. The fountain itself was composed of three porticos of gilded iron, with large jets in the center of each, while seven jets leaped up from the basins above the porticos, and all the waters rushed down over the steps of marble. In addition, twenty-two vases at the sides of the bosquet threw jets into the air."

It was not always possible for the king to do as he wished, however, and many in the court were not pleased to be asked to move from their comfortable Parisian homes to a wooded area several miles away that was more suited for hunting than balls. One courtier, Madame de Sévigné, complained on October 12, 1678, "The King, wishes to go on Saturday to Versailles, but it seems that God does not wish it, by the impossibility of putting the buildings in a state to receive him, and by the great mortality among the workmen."

By then, Louis was also distracted by his other favorite pastime: fighting to expand his kingdom. Joining other nations, including former enemies Sweden and England, he went to war against the Dutch Republic, and this time, France was more successful than in the previous War of Devolution. In 1678, he signed the Treaty of Nijmegen, which ended the war against the Dutch and gained him Burgundy.

The treaty also allowed him to return to working on his palatial home, and Hardouin-Mansart went to work on the famed Hall of Mirrors, a long and impressive structure of glass that connects two pavilions, known respectively as the Salon of Peace and the Salon of War. The Hall of Mirrors overlooked the famed fountains, of which one contemporary chronicler wrote, "Nothing is more surprising than the immense quantity of water thrown up by the fountains when they all play together at the promenades of the King. These jets are capable of using up a river." Another author, writing centuries later, described the scene: "To the east, beyond the brilliant parterre of Latona, with its fountains, its flowers, and its orange-trees, rise the vine-covered walls of the terraces, with their spacious flights of steps and their vividly green clipped yews…Turn to the west and survey the Royal Allée, the Basin of Apollo, and the Grand Canal, or look to the north to the Allée of Ceres, or to the south to that of Bacchus, and you realize the harmony that existed between Mansart and Le Nôtre in the decoration of the chateau and in the plan of the gardens."

Myra Bella's picture of the Hall of Mirrors

Hardouin-Mansart also worked to design the Orangerie, a citrus garden that continues to impress visitors who come to Versailles today. In addition to the obvious citrus trees, introduced to Europe in the 1500s, Hardouin-Mansart also planted palm and oleander trees, as well as olive and pomegranate trees. What makes all these trees most interesting is that they were planted in large boxes and remained in hot houses for most of the year, so they were only brought out during the warm summer months. The king's gardeners were able to use special techniques to keep the trees blooming year round.

By 1682, Versailles had begun to look somewhat like what it does today. The king's personal quarters took up the entire north side of the new building, both first and second floors, while the queen's apartments took up the of the southern half of the first floor, with the royal children living above her. It is interesting to note that the king and queen's apartments were equal in size, which was unusual during that era. Some historians speculate that he honored his queen in this way not out of affection but instead out of ambition, for he hoped to put his wife on the throne of Spain. In fact, he had fought the War of Devolution to this end, hoping to overthrow his father-in-law and thus rule both countries.

The two royal apartments were part of a suite of seven rooms, each decorated to honor one of the Greco-Roman deities. A prize had been offered back in 1663 to anyone who could come up with an appropriate décor for these all important chambers, and when the winner was announced, those in charge observed, "As for the proposal to depict the heroic actions of the King, it has been resolved that he shall be painted and depicted in the form of Danaus in such a way as to fit the story of the conquest of Dunkirk." One contemporary writer insisted, "These subjects were chosen with the King in mind...No sooner had he taken the government of his State in hand than His Majesty, preoccupied with the happiness of his subjects, began to promote commerce with the most remote places, and to that end dispatched French colonists to Madagascar and various other countries; for this is what truly inspired these paintings."

In *Realms of Memory: The Construction of the French Past*, the authors wrote, "Artists were thus well versed in the use of 'parallels' when the decoration of the king's apartments began. In the Salon of Diana, the four paintings that frame the central motif depict Cyrus attacking a boar; Alexander hunting for lion; Caesar sending colonists to Carthage; and Jason approaching Colchos in his quest for the Golden Fleece...the ceilings of the king's apartments are a veritable illustrated textbook of the first ten years of Louis XIV's personal reign. They display the virtues of the monarchs, his diplomatic successes, the development of the navy and of commerce, the patronage accorded to literature and the sciences and the construction projects undertaken by the regime."

Meanwhile, a terrace ran along the western portion of the "enveloppe," as the "castle around a castle" was known. Versaille also had something entirely revolutionary: the appartement des bains featured a sunken tub and hot and cold running water. As was the custom, other royals joined the king and his immediate family in the palace, with the Duke and Duchess of Orleans, his brother and sister-in-law, living in apartments in the southern part of the new addition.

One of Versailles' most noteworthy features around that time was the Trianon de Porcelain (the Porcelain Pavilion), a large, elegantly columned chateau where the king could entertain. Started in 1670, it was paved with thousands of blue and white ceramic tiles from France's best tile makers. However, within just a few years of the pavilion's completion in 1672, the tiles had begun to crack and fade, and by 1687, they looked so bad that Louis ordered his workmen to tear down the pavilion and rebuild it with something that would last longer. Thus, Hardouin-Mansart created a bigger and better pavilion using red marble. The second pavilion, known from then on as the Grand Trianon, was completed in 1687.

A 1700 portrait of the Grand Trianon

M. Konnikara's pictures of the Grand Trianon

Some years later, Louis' sister-in-law wrote of her stay there, "My lodgings are excellent; I have four rooms and an office, whence I am writing to you now. I have a view of the Springs, as they call them. The Springs are set in a little grove which is so densely covered that even the midday sun can't get in. There are more than fifty springs flowing up from the ground, forming little streams barely a foot wide, which are easy to step over; they are lined with grass, making little islands just big enough for a table and two chairs, so you can play cards there in the shade…There are steps on either side, because the whole thing is sloped…; the water flows down the steps too, making waterfalls on either side. As you can imagine, it's a very agreeable spot."

While some people, especially ladies, were invited to stay at the Grand Trianon, it was primarily designed as a place for Louis to "get away from it all." One 19th century historian explained, "In the midst of all the austerities imposed upon him by the ambition of Madame de Maintenon, the King went to Trianon to inhale the breath of the flowers which he had planted there, of the rarest and most odoriferous kind. On the infrequent occasions when the Court was permitted to accompany him thither to share in his evening collation, it was a beautiful spectacle to see so many charming women wandering in the midst of the flowers on the terrace rising from the banks of the canal…The air was so rich with the mingled perfume of violets, orange flowers, jessamines, tuberoses, hyacinths and narcissuses that the King and his visitors were sometimes obliged to fly from the overpowering sweets. The flowers in the parterres were arranged in a thousand different figures, which were constantly changed, so that one might have supposed it to be the work of some fairy, who, passing over the gardens, threw upon them each time a new robe aglow with color."

Construction continued in Versailles throughout the king's life, causing significant inconvenience for the many living within the palace, and tthe country's poor finances meant that many of the plans for Versailles envisioned by both Le Vau and Hardouin-Mansart were never completed. Louis largely stopped work on Versailles around 1684, with the exception of the construction of a new chapel, but by then, the king and his entire court of 36,000 men and 6,000 horses lived there. As Payne put it, "'The State,' exclaimed the Sun King, 'it is I!' and in the same mood he might have added, 'Versailles--it is the State!'"

Life at Versailles

In addition to the grandeur of the palace, Louis XIV used the move to solidify his power, making Versailles the center of the power in France for years to come. Thousands of courtiers lived in and around the palace, along with their servants, and all matters of state were dealt with there. Louis even insisted all government offices be relocated there and commanded that anyone who wanted to serve in his government must live at the palace for at least a portion of every year. This was a wise move, in that it force landed barons to leave the homes and regions they commanded behind periodically and were thus unable to develop undue influence over their own small fiefdoms. Instead, they were forced to work with the king and other lords in a united, or at least mostly united, government.

The nobility lived in apartments and rooms at the palace, which ranged from great suites of rooms near the king to small, cramped quarters. Those who had higher social status were naturally afforded the better accommodations closer to the king, while attic apartments and those far from the king were the lowest status. Larger apartments were spread over more than a single floor, including large rooms for bathing, reception rooms, dining spaces and bedrooms.

Although Versailles is Europe's most famous palace and the epitome of luxury and wealth, it was not nearly as majestic in the 17th century as it seems to be today. Construction at the palace was constant, even after 1684 (when the major projects were stopped), with rooms being redecorated and repaired constantly. Ladies constantly complained of the mess and wet plaster everywhere, and though the palace was built on a grand scale, little attention was paid to matters of hygiene. Servants and others even relieved themselves in the halls of Versailles, causing a horrible odor throughout the palace.

Court rituals in particular busied the nobility. Each morning, they vied to attend the king at his leve or rising, and they vied to attend his couche in the evening. Similar formal rituals were enacted in the queen's chamber each day. Louis' formally scheduled day impacted the entire court, from the king down to the lowliest servants. Meals, like rising and retiring, were formal and public, with courtiers spending much of their time trying to get as close to the king, Queen or other significant members of the royal family as possible. It was said of the vain Sun King that flattery was the quickest way to his good graces, all the better if the means of flattery were personally embarrassing. One courtier of the king, Saint-Simon, noted, "There was nothing he liked so much as flattery, or, to put it more plainly, adulation; the coarser and clumsier it was, the more he relished it". Still, there was good reason to put on such theatrics: favor from the king meant not only improved quarters at Versailles, but also the likelihood of a life-long appointment to a position that would bring wealth and status.

Given the king's fondness for arts and culture, the court required art, architecture and entertainment. Theatricals, comedies and ballets were common. Louis' love of the ballet continued throughout his life, and he continued to dance in court ballets for many years, until his final performance in 1670. He also patronized several significant playwrights of the seventeenth century, including Moliere. For his own performances, Louis chose the most glorious characters, favoring, in particular Apollo, the classical sun god. The artwork at Versailles also creates the impression of a god-like ruler, as statues speaking to classical themes adorned Versailles.

Perhaps not surprisingly, Louis remained ever-conscious of his personal appearance. As a young man, Louis was considered to be extraordinarily handsome and quite vain. When he moved the court to Versailles, the court rituals were elaborately based around his dress, and he began to even regulate court dress, requiring everyone to meet his high standards. As he aged, he continued to ride and hunt, remaining fit well into what by a 17th century definition qualified as old age. The Sun King was in his 50s before he began to put on weight and show his age, and even still his clothing was impeccably tailored and made from the finest cloth. When he began to go bald, he made wigs a fashionable choice for men at court and was not seen without his.

As the importance of appearances and rituals at Versailles suggests, Louis also implemented strict rules for those who lived there. Margaret Visser wrote in *Of Versailles and France,* "During the 17th century, in France, manners became a political issue. King Louis XIV and his predecessors…instituted a sort of school of manners. At the palace, the courtiers lived under the despotic surveillance of the king, and upon their good behavior, their deference, and their observance of etiquette their whole careers depended. If you displeased a Louis, he would simply "not see you" the following day; his gaze would pass over you as he surveyed the people before him. And not being "seen" by the king was tantamount to ceasing to count, at Versailles…A whole timetable of ceremonies was followed, much of it revolving around the King's own person. Intimacy with Louis meant power, and power was symbolically expressed in attending to certain of the king's most private and physical needs: handing him his stockings to put on in the morning, being present as he used to chaise percée, rushing when the signal sounded to be present as he got ready for bed…The point about Versailles was that there was no escape: the courtiers had to 'make it' where they were. The stage was Louis's, and the roles that could be played were designed by him. It was up to each courtier to fit him- or herself into one of the slots provided. The leaders of all the other towns and villages of France were made…to feel their subordination, the distance from the court."

The Duchess of Orleans provided insight into what life was like at court in a letter to a friend on January 4, 1704, complaining, "The Duchesse de Bourgogne's ladies…tried to arrogate the rank and take the place of my ladies everywhere. Such a thing was never done either in the time of the Queen or of the Dauphiness. They got the King's Guards to keep their places and push back the chairs belonging to my ladies. I complained first of all to the Duc de Noailles, who replied that it was the King's order. Then I went immediately to the King and said to him, 'May I ask your Majesty if it is by your orders that my ladies have now no place or rank as they used to have? The King became quite red, and replied, 'I have given no such order, who said that I had?' 'The Maréchal de Noailles,' I replied. The King asked him why he had said such a thing, and he denied it entirely. 'I am willing to believe, since you say so,' I replied, 'that my lackey misunderstood you, but as the King has given no such orders, see that your Guards don't keep places for those ladies and hinder my servants from carrying chairs for my service,' as we say here. Although these ladies are high in favour, the King, nevertheless, sent the majordomo to find out how things should be done. I told him, and it will not happen again. These women are becoming far too insolent now that they are in favour, and they imagined that I would not have the courage to report the matter to the King. But I shall not lose my rank nor prerogatives on account of the favour they enjoy. The King is too just for that."

When he was not preoccupied with ensuring that those around him behaved properly, Louis was busy with the fifth and final phase of his work on Versailles. In 1697, he suffered a sound defeat in the War of the League of Augsburg. Likely depressed over this loss, he turned to his home for solace. This time, however, his priorities were different; whereas in the past the Sun King had focused his efforts on his own comfort and entertainment, this time the aging king was working toward something more "eternal." He had Hardouin-Mansart design a royal chapel for his palace, a place where he likely hoped to make his peace with God. Writing for the *World Heritage Guide*, Jerome Sabatier observed, "The Royal Chapel, designed by Hardouin-Mansart, is dedicated to Louis IX. Completed in 1710, Louis XIV would only use this chapel during the last five years of his life. The kings of France were thought to have been chosen by God as his representative on Earth, a concept known as the divine right of kings…The configuration and decoration of the chapel reflect this idea. Thus, the passion of Christ, the Resurrection and the descent of the Holy Spirit, thought to inspire the accomplishments and actions of the king, are addressed in a carefully prepared and beautifully executed series of paintings and structures in the chapel. The King and his family attended Mass every day at 10 a.m., and sat in the royal gallery."

The exterior of the chapel

A depiction of Louis XIV praying before the chapel

Brian Jeffery Beggarly's picture of the chapel's altar

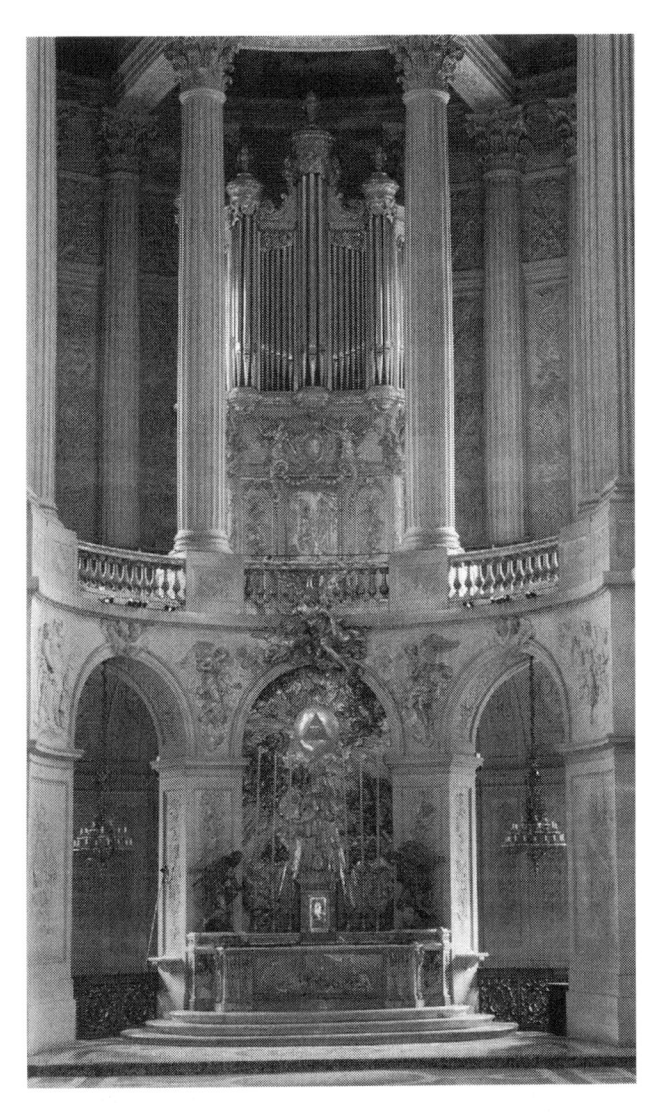

Maximillian Puhane's picture of the chapel's organ

Louis spent more than a decade supervising every detail of the chapel's construction, and when it was completed in 1710, so was Versailles as a whole, for the most part. Imbert de Saint-Amand noted at the time, "There is an intimate relation between the King and his château. The idol is worthy of the temple, the temple of the idol. There is always something immaterial, something moral so to speak, in monuments, and they derive their poesy from the thought connected with them. For a cathedral, it is the idea of God. For Versailles, it is the idea of the King. Its mythology is but a magnificent allegory of which Louis XIV is the reality…It is he always and everywhere. Fabulous heroes and divinities impart their attributes to him or mingle with his courtiers. In honor of him, Neptune sheds broadcast the waters that cross in air in sparkling arches. Apollo, his favorite symbol, presides over this enchanted world as the god of light, the inspirer of the muses; the sun of the god seems to pale before that of the great King. Nature and art combine to celebrate the glory of the sovereign by a perpetual hosanna…All that generations of kings have amassed in pictures, statues and precious movables is distributed as mere furniture in the glittering apartments of the chateau. The intoxicating perfumes of luxury and power throw one into a sort of ecstasy that makes comprehensible the exaltation of this monarch, enthusiastic over himself, who, in chanting the hymns composed in his praise, shed tears of admiration."

The Influence of Versailles

While Louis XIV's palace still stands, the Sun King died in 1715. Preceded in death by all of his six children, and by his grandson, he left the throne to his five year old great-grandson, Louis XV. Young Louis XV's regent, Philippe II, Duke of Orleans, wasted no time moving the French court back to Paris and rarely used Versailles.

Philippe II, Duke of Orleans

Louis XV

While Versailles fell out of favor with French leaders in the 1710s, outsiders were still fascinated by it. The famous Russian Tsar Peter the Great stayed in the Grand Trianon when he visited France in May 1717. In fact, he made the visit specifically to study the palace and gardens to gain ideas for his own palace, Peterhof, which he was working on. According to one of his biographers, Linsey Hughes, "[A]t Versailles on 14 May he inspected the gardens and fountains on the first of several visits. He spent the night in Madam de Maintenon's rooms in the Trianon, where her old servant was horrified by the Russians' bad behavior. On 30 May he was back at Versailles for his birthday, when fireworks and illuminations were organized at Marly and torches and lamps were brought from Paris to light up the Agrippina found, his favorite…These visits and twelve albums of engravings of Versailles which he received as a gift from the royal library provided ample material for extending his own Palaces at Peterhof and Strel'na, which he visited with new enthusiasm after the trip to Paris."

Peter the Great

When Louis XV reached his majority in 1721, he immediately began to make plans to return to Versailles, and he moved the court there in 1722. Once there, he showed that he was indeed a Bourbon King by starting a new building project, albeit one that in no way rivaled those of his famed predecessor. He was troubled that the Salon of Hercules, which was begun during the last years of his great-grandfather's life, had never been finished, so he made it his personal project to see it completed. Pierre de Nolhac, who served as director of the Versailles Museum in the late 19th century, explained, "The enormous marble chimney-piece by Autin is loaded with bronzes, in the middle of which is a head of Hercules, covered with the lion's skin. We are in the famous Hall of Hercules, and the ceiling…represents the apotheosis of Hercules and his reception among the gods of Olympus. This painting, which is the work of Louis XV's first painter Lemoyne, and is his masterpiece, was completed in the six years between 1729 and 1736. It is the largest surface that has ever been covered by single composition in France…It is said that the painter was greatly complimented by the King and Court when his work, so long hidden by scaffolding, was disclosed to view; but his expenses in colors and accessories had been so high that the honorarium of ten thousand écus did not cover them. He had spent twenty-four thousand francs in ultramarine alone! The unfortunate artist, not daring to put forward any claim, killed himself in despair." When it was completed, the room featured "the *Feast at the House of Simon the Pharisee*, by Paul Veronese...For this great picture, presented to Louis XIV, by the Republic of Venice, the carver Vassé made the large carved frame...."

Louis XV also added some smaller apartments for himself and his family members, perhaps overwhelmed by the massive places in which his great-grandfather lived. But his most lasting contribution was the Petit Trianon. In *Architecture of France,* David A. Hanser told readers, "The Petiti Trianon was relatively small for an aristocratic residence. It is square, about 86 feet on a side, though because of the extremely thick exterior and interior stones walls, not all of the roughly 7,400 square feet per floor is usable. It was conventional in number and size of rooms: a large dining room, a music room, two other small rooms for receiving and entertaining guests, and a bedroom suite on the main floor; thirteen guests rooms on the attic floor above; and formal entry on the floor below...All this was appropriate for a king who wanted occasionally to live like an upper-class gentlemen instead of in the midst of hundreds of courtiers and servants." In this case, it meant that the king would live with his mistress, Madame de Pompadour. Hanser continued, "Madame de Pompadour...convinced Louis XV to build the Petit Trianon. Around 1750, she had encouraged the king...to create a series of experimental gardens...near the Grand Trianon. In 1753, a temporary pavilion was built near the botanical gardens for meals. It was so successful that in 1761, the king commission a more permanent structure from Gabriel." Ironically, de Pompadour died four years before her home was completed, and so Madame de Barry, who succeeded her as the king's romantic interest, lived there instead. Nonetheless, "It is the masterpiece of Anges-Jacques Gabriel, one of the greatest European architects of the eighteenth century. He had succeeded his father as First Architect to the king in 1742, and remained in that position until the day after Louis XV...died in 1774."

Writing of the Petit Trianon in 1961, authors Edwin Smith and Sacheverell Sitwell described it as having "[f]ive plain, high, unadorned windows; five even simpler, smaller ones above them; four columns; a terrace and some steps: with these few features, Gabriel has made a faultless work of art. One cannot say, 'If only it had urns on the top!', 'If only it had more carving round the windows!'. It lacks nothing. Least of all can one say, 'If only it were larger!'...Walking clockwise around it, one sees the north front; five tall windows with five small windows above; four columns; above these, the balustrade; below, the terrace. The even greater simplicity in line is compensated by more elaboration in the carving of the stone. The east side, compared to the others, is disappointing: but one can at least see that another side of the box has been treated differently and with even greater simplicity. Continuing clockwise, one comes, illogically perhaps, to the entrance, and then any doubts about Gabriel's genius and invention are dispelled...The walls of the little courtyard lead up to a simple ground floor; on this solid support stand five tall windows, five smaller ones above, four columns and the balustrade: the same wall-space, the same fenestration but a completely different variation on the same theme. What Mozart could do in music, Gabriel has done in stone."

Myra Bella's picture of the Petit Trianon

A picture of the dining room inside

Pleased with Gabriel's work, Louis commissioned him to update the facades in the palace' courtyard in a more classical design. This work continued under Louis XVI but was interrupted by the French Revolution and was not completed until the 20th century.

All these building projects took up space, and even the great Versailles had only so much space, so Louis XV ordered the famed Ambassador's Stair, the elegant public entrance to the State Apartments, torn down to make room for his daughters. This move is somewhat symbolic of what was happening within the royal family at that time, as Louis XV was more interested in his own comfort and pleasure, and that of his family, than he was in matters of state.

When Louis XVI ascended the throne in 1774, he was only 20 years old. His queen, the now infamous Marie Antoinette, was just as young. Together they set out to make Versailles something of a faux pastoral paradise, focusing their attention on the gardens around the palace rather than the building itself. Louis ordered the trees that had died since the time of Louis XIV replaced, and he replaced the Labyrinthe with a smaller garden for his personal use. Inside the palace, the young queen took the lead, having her own apartments and those of her husband redecorated.

Louis XVI at the age of 20

Marie Antoinette

The doomed queen's apartments were lavishly decorated with every comfort and convenience, including, according to one report, "tables for writing, and two chests of drawers of elaborate workmanship. The curtains and hangings were of rich but plain blue silk. The stools for those that had the privilege of being seated in the royal presence, with a sofa for the Queen's use, were placed against the walls, according to the formal custom of the time. The canopy of the bed was adorned with Cupids playing with garlands and holding gilt lilies, the royal flower."

In the early years of their reign, the new king and queen enjoyed visits from dignitaries from around the world, among them Dr. Benjamin Franklin, whose well-known wit charmed and amused them. For his part, Franklin later wrote to his landlady back in Philadelphia, "We went to Versailles last Sunday, and had the honor of being presented to the King, Louis XV. In the evening we were at the 'Grand Convert,' where the family sup in public. The table was half a hollow square, the service of gold…Versailles has had infinite sums laid out in building it and supplying it with water. Some say the expenses exceeded eighty millions sterling

($400,000,000). The range of buildings is immense; the garden-front most magnificent, all of hewn stone; the number of statues, figures, urns, etc., in marble and bronze of exquisite workmanship, is beyond conception."

At the same time, Franklin was able to spot several signs of decay, noting, "But the water-works are out of repair, and so is a great part of the front next the town, looking, with its shabby, half-brick walls, and broken windows, not much better than the houses in Durham Yard. There is, in short, both at Versailles and Paris, a prodigious mixture of magnificence and negligence with every kind of elegance except that of cleanliness, and what we call tidiness."

The part of the palace most closely associated with Marie Antoinette and her eventual fall from grace was the Petit Trianon, which Louis gave her for her own personal use. It was here that she kept sheep and played the farmer's daughter, often dressing in simple frocks and entertaining friends of various characters, even as the French public grew restless. Louis XVI and Marie Antoinette did not fully grasp that the days of monarchs living in grand palaces distant from the vast majority of their subjects, many of whom lived in squalor, were rapidly coming to an end.

On October 6, 1789, the royal family finally had to face the reality of what was going on around them. Following the Women's March on Versailles, during which women from around the city converged on the palace to complain about the high price of bread, Louis XVI and his family left Versailles for the last time. From that point on, the citizens in and around the town were in charge of the palace's preservation.

In October 1790, Louis ordered his servants to move the furniture from the palace to the Tuileries Palace, where he and the rest of the royals were living, but the Mayor of Versailles protested this move, noting that the city had already suffered a terrible loss in population when the court left. He understandably feared that if the king removed the furniture from the premises, it would signal that he was certainly not coming back, and the surrounding area would soon fall into ruin. When a committee from the town presented this letter to Louis XVI on October 12, he rescinded his previous order, and the furniture remained in place.

As fate would have it, the king would never see his possessions again. Instead, on June 21, 1791, Louis was arrested, and all of the possessions he owned were declared by the National Constituent Assembly to have been abandoned.

On January 21, 1793, the deposed king was brought before the guillotine, an instrument of death he had helped bring about. If Louis had any thoughts about the manner in which he was to die, they may very well have been ones of relief, for he had no doubt read about other unfortunate nobles who had been the victims of botched executions. At least the guillotine would likely do its job quickly, if not cleanly.

For this occasion, the guillotine was moved to the Place de Louis XV, named for the doomed king's own grandfather. Father Henry Essex Edgeworth accompanied the king on his final journey and later recalled, "As soon as the King had left the carriage…he undressed himself, untied his neckcloth, opened his shirt, and arranged it himself. The guards…surrounded him again, and would have seized his hands. 'What are you attempting?' said the King, drawing back his hands. 'To bind you,' answered the wretches. 'To bind me,' said the King, with an indignant air. 'No! I shall never consent to that: do what you have been ordered, but you shall never bind me. . .'"

. Louis made his way to the scaffold with difficulty but finally arrived and stood one last time. Ironically, he was placed near a pedestal that had previously held a statue of his grandfather, Louis XV. Allowed to speak, Louis told his former subjects, "I die perfectly innocent of the so-called crimes of which I am accused. I pardon those who are the cause of my misfortunes."

Though he wished to say more, he was cut off by a drum roll ordered by Antoine-Joseph Santerre, a general in the National Guard. According to Edgeworth, "He was proceeding, when a man on horseback, in the national uniform, and with a ferocious cry, ordered the drums to beat. Many voices were at the same time heard encouraging the executioners. They seemed reanimated themselves, in seizing with violence…they dragged him under the axe of the guillotine, which with one stroke severed his head from his body. All this passed in a moment."

Then came the final step: "The youngest of the guards, who seemed about eighteen, immediately seized the head, and showed it to the people as he walked round the scaffold; he accompanied this monstrous ceremony with the most atrocious and indecent gestures. At first an awful silence prevailed; at length some cries of 'Vive la Republique!' were heard. By degrees the voices multiplied and in less than ten minutes this cry, a thousand times repeated became the universal shout of the multitude, and every hat was in the air."

Prudhomme, who had served as the third Charles Sanson's deputy, later described the melee that followed: "Some individuals steeped their handkerchiefs in his blood. A number of armed volunteers crowded also to dip in the blood of the despot their pikes, their bayonets, or their sabres. Several officers of the Marseillese battalion, and others, dipped the covers of letters in this impure blood, and carried them on the points of their swords at the head of their companies, exclaiming 'This is the blood of a tyrant!'"

An even more sickening gesture followed, according to Prudhomme: "One citizen got up to the guillotine itself, and, plunging his whole arm into the blood of Capet, of which a great quantity remained, he took up handfuls of the clotted gore, and sprinkled it over the crowd below which pressed round the scaffold, each anxious to receive a drop on his forehead. 'Friends,' said this citizen, in sprinkling them, 'we were threatened that the blood of Louis should be on our heads; and so you see it is!'"

A contemporary depiction of King Louis XVI's execution

Marie Antoinette, now called the Widow Capet or simply Antoinette, was devastated by the loss of her husband. In early 1793, even while she continued to hope for a possible exchange of prisoners or release, her health began to deteriorate. It is believed she may have been suffering from the early stages of both tuberculosis and uterine cancer, and she saw the doctor for convulsions and fainting fits.

Marie Antoinette

Already failing, Antoinette was devastated by the removal of her son in early July 1793, and the former queen was herself arrested and transferred to the prison at the Palais du Justice during the night of August 1, 1793. While her cell in the prison was less luxurious, the more public accommodations allowed her access to priests and others. Her jailers were kind and even relatively indulgent, allowing her good quality food, mineral water, and access to books. A plot to free the Queen in early September led to somewhat harsher conditions as well as long interrogations.

While she conducted herself well under duress, the decision had already been made, and her "trial" was even more of a sham than her husband's. The revolutionary government saw the former queen's execution as essential to cement their place and unify the revolutionaries. To that end, the former Queen was accused of a host of trumped up charges, including throwing orgies in Versailles, sending millions of livres to Austria, plotting to assassinate the Duke of Orléans, having her Swiss Guards massacred in 1792, and, worst of all, sexually abusing her son. To that end, her young son was coached by authorities to turn against her and level charges of sexual abuse. While she was allowed legal counsel, she was given less than a day to prepare a defense against charges whose origins came from libelles, the 18th century equivalent of tabloids.

Antoinette remained composed during the proceedings until pressed about the sexual abuse charge leveled against her. To that point, when asked why she had remained silent regarding that charge, the doting mother countered, "If I have not replied it is because Nature itself refuses to respond to such a charge laid against a mother." After more than 30 hours of trial over two days, Antoinette was convicted and sentenced to death. She was allowed pen and paper to write a letter to her sister-in-law Elisabeth, but she was not granted a priest to make her final confession or privacy to change her clothing. In her letter to Elisabeth, she wrote of her clear conscience and her love for her children, but the letter would never reach Élisabeth.

On October 16, 1793, the former queen had her hair cut off and was paraded through Paris on an open cart. The woman placed into the cart for the final journey to the guillotine was nothing like the young girl who had come to Versailles. By now, the Widow Capet was thin, pale, and suffering from serious blood loss as the result of her gynecological difficulties. Nevertheless, she remained quiet and dignified on the cart ride and as she mounted the scaffold, her courage intact. Her last words were reputed to have been "Pardon me sir, I meant not to do it," after she had inadvertently stepped on her executioner's toe while mounting the scaffold.

Descriptions of the queen's death were much less dramatic than that of her husband. According to the *Edinburgh Advertiser* of November 12, 1793, "She ascended the scaffold with seeming haste and impatience; and then turned her eyes with great emotion towards the garden of the Tuileries, the former abode of her greatness. At half past twelve o'clock, the Guillotine severed her head from her body. ... When her head was under the fatal axe, she was heard to exclaim, 'Adieu, my Children! I go to your Father!'"

A depiction of Marie Antoinette's execution

By the time Marine Antoinette was executed, Versailles had been sealed. On August 23, 1793, just a few months before her death, the Assembly began auctioning off most of Versailles' contents. A few particularly important items were kept for museums, but everything else was gone by January 19, 1795.

At first, it seemed that Versailles itself would be sold, but the Assembly, having killed just about everyone who would have had the time and resources to maintain such a palace during the Reign of Terror, decided to keep it as a public museum. In the years that followed, the revolutionaries destroyed a number of churches and private homes, often moving the art and other valuables from their rightful owners to the museum at Versailles.

As a result, Versailles was slowly reborn into a new cultural center. In June 1794, the sieur Fayolle became the first Director of Conservation for the museum, and the following year, public administrator and people's representative Andre Dumont took over supervision of the physical parts of the building and the grounds. Appalled with the state of disrepair that the palace and the grounds had so quickly fallen into, Dumont worked quickly to put together a team of conservators, repairmen, and gardeners to restore it to, if not its former glory, at least a functioning facility. To that end, Dumont appointed Huges Lagarde to catalogue the more than 200,000 books and manuscripts left behind in the palace. Thrilled by what he found behind the closed doors of the library and other rooms, Lagarde expanded his efforts to include Fayolle, whom he put in charge of gathering and curating natural history items, and the painter Louis Jean-Jacques Durameau, who had painted the ceiling of the Opera at Versailles, to handle the paintings.

In 1797, Versailles was designated the Special Museum of the French School. Lagarde had the largest apartments turned into art galleries, where paintings and sculptures by French artists were displayed. Among the most famous pieces was the Peter Paul Rubens' *Life of Marie de Medicis*, and over time, the museum developed the finest collection of classic French art in the world.

Unfortunately, there was only so much that Lagarde and his team could do, especially with all the upheaval going on in the country in the wake of the French Revolution and the start of the Napoleonic Era. Versailles was constantly being cannibalized, with its mirrors being used to pay off debts and its beautiful drapes and upholstery being harvested for their gold and silver threads. In the fall of 1799, some of the former kings' own apartments were turned over to doctors and surgeons to house wounded soldiers.

Napoleon was a man of war, not peace, and when he came to power, he broke up Versailles' vast collections and ordered that the pieces be shipped to various other locations for display. He then turned Versailles into a government palace and made it the capitol of Seine-et-Oise, a municipality encompassing most of Paris. Napoleon himself lived in the Grand Trianon, while his empress, the beautiful and accomplished Marie-Louise, had apartments in the palace itself. All the while, much of the palace continued to be used as a veteran's hospital.

Napoleon

Of course, Napoleon himself did not remain in power for long. After Waterloo forced Napoleon into exile again, it paved the way for the Bourbon Restoration, but Louis XVII and Louis XVIII were both desperately interested in keeping their thrones and their heads, so they did little to make waves during their reigns. They had some work done on the gardens at Versailles but left the rooms largely as they found them. It is said that Louis XVIII would sometimes secretly visit Versailles and wander through the empty rooms, looking perhaps for scenes of faded glory. His successor, Charles X, lived at the Tuileries and visited the great Versailles only on special occasions.

Louis XVIII

Upheaval struck again in 1830 when Louis-Philippe I overthrew his more conservative relatives and made himself king of France. Unlike his predecessors, he had big plans for the palace, and in March 1832 he declared it a crown dependency. Writing in 1839, Leitch Ritchie explained, "When Louis Philippe first cast his eye upon Versailles, after his accession to the throne, he saw at once the impiety of allowing such a monument to sink into utter ruin. ... He felt that the day of the great king had passed by; that the monarchical power was now in alliance with the popular power; and that the nation, in which both were combined, was the only paramount idea left by the revolution of July...He determined that the palace of Louis XIV, without losing its individuality, should become a palace of the entire people; and that the bygone spirit of absolutism should give shelter, as it were, to the spirit of modern liberty. Versailles, therefore, erected as a homage to individual pride, has become, under the Orleans regime, a great national monument — and certainly the most complete and splendid of its class in all Europe…To carry out this idea, immense alterations were requisite in the interior of the palace. Numbers of small rooms were thrown into one; and the holes and corners of Versailles were visited with the light of day, which shamed, without banishing, their voluptuous associations. The temple of luxury was converted into a temple of the arts, and French valour recorded in immortal colors upon the walls, by French genius. The whole edifice is one vast museum. Every room is a gallery of pictures or statues ; and there is still to be added a collection of national models."

Louis-Philippe I

In the decade that followed, Frédéric Nepveu and Pierre-François-Léonard Fontaine worked together to convert the palace from a home for a king to a museum for his people. Louis-Philippe opened it in connection with his son's marriage, tying the public and private lives of the royals together in a way that would have impressed even Louis XIV. But Louis-Philippe went a step further than just establishing a museum; he established how visitors should tour his museum, including the following instructions:

> "The visitor will go to the baths of Apollo, and consider them, as well as the fountain and the rails ; and after having made the tour, he will go to Flora."

> "He will afterwards pass by Ceres to go to the theatre, and will see the changes, and consider the jets of the cascades."

> "He will go out by the dragon, and pass by the alley of children; and on arriving at a stone which is between the two basins below, he will turn round to take a peep at all the jets of Neptune and the dragon, and then continue to ascend by the said abbey."

To be fair to Louis-Philippe, there was so much to see that he might be reasonably concerned that visitors would become overwhelmed. In the southern wing housed the Hall of Battles, created by removing most of the apartments formerly set aside for royal family members and visitors. The Hall of Battles focused on French victories spanning over a millennium, from the Battle of Tolbiac (c. 495) to the Battle of Wagram on July 5-6, 1809. Here visitors could marvel at the *Battle of Taillebourg* by Eugène Delacroix before moving on to the Salle des Croisades, dedicated to the French Knights who had fought in the Crusades. Later, they could tour the portrait galleries created by tearing down walls between the rooms set aside for the king's children.

Ultimately, Louis Napoleon took power in 1852. As Emperor Napoleon III, he undertook an extensive building program that included the famed Paris Opera House. He was also a great patron of the arts, but he did little to influence the way in which the museum of Versailles was run, aside from using the museum as a backdrop for his own triumphs and entertainments.

Napoleon III

While most museums are only open during traditional business hours, there is nothing like touring one in the evening, and on one special night in August 1855, Versailles offered quite a sight. One writer described the scene: "[T]he grand court of the château shone with a brilliance resembling day. The profile of the great edifice was outlined in small lights. In the gardens, arches and columns were raised and the fountains showered rainbow torrents. The Hall of Mirrors presented a spectacle whose splendor recalled nights when Louis XIV strolled here in brocade and ruffles. Garlands hung from the ceiling, thousands of lights reproduced themselves in the lofty mirrors and shed scintillating floods upon the handsome costumes of the invited ones."

It seems that throughout France's history, it was the destiny of Versailles to rise and fall with the nation. Thus, in 1870, when the Germans defeated France in the Franco-Prussian War and lay siege to Paris, Versailles became the Prussian army's main headquarters. In fact, Wilhelm I was proclaimed Emperor of the new German Empire in the Hall of Mirrors on January 18, 1871. One chronicler noted, "It was impossible for the boldest imagination to picture a more thorough revenge on the traditional foes of Germany than the proclamation of the German Empire in the storied palace of the Kings of France. With the shades of Richelieu and the Grand Monarch looking down upon them did the Teutonic chieftains raise as it were, their leader on their shields, and with clash of arms and martial music acclaim him kaiser of a re-united Germany."

Proclamation of the German Empire, 18 January 1871, 1877 **by Anton von Werner**

With the Germans once more driven from the city, order was restored to both Paris and Versailles, and in 1887, Pierre de Nolhac came to work at the museum. Five years later, on November 18, 1892, he was appointed its curator, and he had big plans for renovating and revitalizing the center. He announced that he would be re-opening the historical galleries, but with a more scientific and orderly routine than the one favored by Louis-Philippe I. Nolhac also began an extensive rebuilding project on Versailles itself, trying to restore at least some rooms to what they had been before they had been remodeled.

Pierre de Nolhac

His hard work paid off in a surprising way, for on Christmas Eve in 1894, the *Associated Press* reported, "Under the dust accumulated in years on the woodwork of a corridor in the palace of Versailles M. Pierre de Nolhac has had the good fortune to discover paintings of great beauty, executed in the time of Marie Antoinette. They are on a cream tinted background, basket of flowers, landscapes, and rustic scenes, framed in blue borders, Louis XV in style. Around the panels are garlands ascribed to the Dauphin's Austrian taste...Louis Philippe, who liked only white and gilt decorations, was the bourgeois king who caused these works to be recovered with whitewash, and yet the Romanticists thought they had, in 1848, exhausted all subjects of complaint against him."

Nolhac was not just a master of art and architecture but also something of a marketing genius who was was able to draw both national and international celebrities to the museum for tours. Eugénie de Montijo, the wife of Napoleon III, visited Versailles, as did the ill-fated Tsar Nicholas II and his wife. In 1907, Nolhac created the Friends of Versailles to honor generous donors, including American newspaper magnate James Gordon Bennett, whose 25,000 franc donation paid for much of the work done on some of the palace's older rooms.

Like the White House in America and Buckingham Palace in England, Versailles continues to serve as a backdrop for official government functions as well. When the French Senate of

National Assembly needs to meet for a unique purpose, such as amending the French Constitution, they leave their more modern meeting rooms and return to Versailles, perhaps in the hopes that they will be inspired by their nation's history. The most famous political event to ever take place at the palace occurred on June 28, 1919, when the United States, France, Great Britain, Italy and Germany, along with other nations, met to sign the famous Treaty of Versailles that ended World War I. It was hoped, that in those golden halls would be born the beginning of world peace, as President Woodrow Wilson told the U.S. Senate the following month: "The treaty constitutes nothing less than a world settlement. It would not be possible for me either to summarize or to construe its manifold provisions in an address which must of necessity be something less than a treatise." He also acknowledged "the problems with which the Peace Conference had to deal and of the difficulty of laying down straight lines of settlement anywhere on a field on which the old lines of international relationship and' the new alike, followed so intricate a pattern and were for the most part cut so deep by historical circumstances which dominated action even where it would have been best to ignore or reverse them…The cross currents of politics and of interest must have been evident to you. It would be presuming in me to attempt to explain the questions which arose or the many diverse elements that entered into them."

Unfortunately, the Treaty of Versailles did not prove to be the panacea of peace that its creators had desired. A generation later, Versailles, along with the rest of Paris, would come under Nazi German occupation in 1940.

World War I, World War II, and the recovery periods after each of them provided very few resources for developing Versailles further. However, in 1952, Gerald Van der Kemp took over as chief conservator for the museum and oversaw some of the most ambitious projects of the 20th century. For instance, in 1957 he completed work on the Opera. When he completed his work, one article described it as "a theatre on the grandest scale…Its vast stage is equaled in all France only by the Paris Opera. Its designers scoured Europe before making their plans and in its day is was one of the technical wonders of the land. When finished it included even a device by which the whole floor of the auditorium could be transformed into a vast banqueting hall or ballroom…But it was a wonder of taste as well. It is elliptical in shape with tiers of boxes and balconies rising from the auditorium supported by sculpted Corinthian columns and embellished with delicately gilded bas reliefs by Augustin Pajou. Its columns were the pinkish shade of Languedoc marble contrasting with the subtle greenish tints of the imitation marble walls…The curtains, chairs and benches were upholstered in turquoise blue silk and dark blue Utrecht velvet, and from the oval ceiling looks down a great painting by Duremeau of Apollo rewarding the arts. A multitude of chandeliers were hung, their brilliance reflected and multiplied by beveled mirrors at the rear of each box. Even in the elegant 18th century, it was a sight to make blasé royal visitors gasp in wonder."

Later, in 1965, Versailles and Van der Kamp's work made the news again when rumors began to circulate that French President Charles de Gaulle was going to make the palace his new home. The *Paris News Service* reported, "General Charles de Gaulle…has ordered the preparation of an official presidential residence at Versailles. …Gen. de Gaulle is not planning to move into the Chateau of Versailles itself, but into the comparatively modest Grand Trianon…. At the ministry, it is emphasized that the Versailles project is designed only incidentally to provide another presidential residence."

The article went on to quote a ministry official, who asserted, "The Trianon is being restored as a 'living museum,' in keeping with the 1962 program for the complete rehabilitation of Versailles. The idea is to create a residence of prestige for state visitors which will be open as a museum when not in official use. Part of the pavilion is being prepared for the head of state so that he can receive his visitors there. … Most of the architectural work will be finished by the end of 1965. Painting and furnishing will take most of 1965…France is spending 80 million francs ($16 million) on restoration of the entire domain of Versailles under a program which began in 1962, with 18 million ($3.6 million) spent in 1964, and an equal amount scheduled for 1965. The amount earmarked for the de Gaulle project has not been made public. …furniture and fabrics are being reproduced to restore the small palace to its appearance in the mid-18th century. " Finally, "Living quarters will be arranged in a long wing called the "Sousbois" where the changes required by modern plumbing will be at least noticed. Much work will be done on the gardens…. However, there are no plans to keep two million pots of flowers on hand for quick changes, as in the days of Louis XIV."

During this period, Van der Kemp also worked on the Northern Wing, converting the first floor into a gallery for paintings depicting scenes from French history. The government took notice and agreed to his pleas for funding to buy back as much as possible of the original furniture and artwork that had been in the palace prior to the French Revolution.

Versailles has remained a popular location for state dinners, and most major world leaders will likely have the opportunity to dine there at least once during any state visit to France. When President Jimmy Carter dined where kings had once supped, the former peanut farmer observed, "We have said many times since arriving in France how closely related our nations have been since the origins of our republics. In addition to the heroism shown by warriors who fought together in times of conflict and trial, we also had intimate relations that existed between the early leaders of our country and the leaders and the people of France." He then added, "It is difficult, perhaps, for citizens of France to know or to comprehend the deep feeling of brotherhood, mutual purpose, and appreciation held in the hearts of Americans for what your nation has done for us…Another characteristic, of course, is the appreciation of beauty. And today we've had a reaffirmation of our consciousness of the beauty that pervades the nation of France—not only the countryside through which we traveled, but this palace, the home that your President has permitted us to use for these two nights. And this afternoon, we had a chance to see the beauty of your artists whom we admire so much in our own country. If France and the United

States, bound so closely together now, can continue to exhibit the bravery and the commitment which we have shown in the past, then human rights will be the historical inevitability of our times."

In the decades since Van der Kemp's time, Versailles has become one of the most popular tourist spots for anyone visiting Paris. In 1989, journalist Michael Matza wrote, "In this land of powerful cultural icons, can there be a more potent symbol of French excess — for good and evil — than the 17th-century chateau that dominates this town of 100,000? Forget all the hype you've heard this year about the French Revolution's bicentennial and stirring reenactments of the storming of the Bastille." He added, "If you want to ride on the road to revolution, skulk the tapestried corridors of power, reflect in the mirrors of the world's most beautiful ballroom and stand your ground where the rabble once roused, then by all means visit Versailles. Any day, any year. It is the story of the rise and fall of absolute monarchy — under one magnificent mansard roof."

Nearly a decade later, in "Visit to Versailles a voluptuous but voracious venture," travel writer Nicholas Woodsworth summed up the magnitude of a modern visit to Versailles: "It was in the Coronation Room, the 17th royal chamber on my tour of the Palace of Versailles, that it struck me that perhaps the celebrated luxury of the court of Louis XIV was not everything it is cracked up to be. Already I had walked through the Hercules Salon, the Abundance Salon, the Venus, Diana, Mars, Mercury and Apollo Salons. I had strolled through the Rooms of War and of Peace, the Great Dining Hall, the King's Guardroom and Marie Antoinette's Bedchamber. I had stumped my way up the Queen's Staircase and down the Prince's Staircase…I was exhausted. I did some quick mathematics. Of a total of 1,250 rooms in the palace, that left 1,233 rooms unseen. Still, there was no doubt about it. Here were some of the most gorgeous, ornate and lavishly appointed interiors that the mind of man, Homo decoratus, had ever imagined. … Some 24 acres of roof-tops cover its sprawling rooms. The Hall of Mirrors alone is an overland trek, 240 feet of endless, echoing magnificence — one needs a map and a packed lunch just to contemplate crossing it."

From October 9, 2008 - January 4, 2009, the Versailles museum hosted a special exhibition of works by American artist Jeff Koons, known for his use of common everyday items in his work. When asked about the setting for his art, he opined, "I hope the juxtaposition of today's surfaces, represented by my work, with the architecture and fine arts of Versailles will be an exciting interaction for the viewer." Speaking on behalf of the museum itself, those in charge of the exhibit insisted, "It is the city aspect that underlies this entire venture. In recent years, many a cultural institution has attempted a confrontation between a heritage setting and contemporary works. The originality of this exhibition seems to us somewhat different, as regards both the chosen venue and the way it has been laid out. Echo, dialectic, opposition, counterpoint…. Not for us to judge!"

It's safe to say that the magnitude and magnificence of Versailles will continue to impress and awe future generations of visitors. One French author may have summed it up best when he mused, "This Versailles, does it not attract to our country strangers without number, does it not lend lasting prestige to the land of France? ... Outside of the Invalides and the Louvre, what edifices equal it in evoking the memorable periods with which they are associated? What lasting respect do these annals of stone and bronze merit from men of taste! These salons, gardens, statues, works of art, attached irrevocably to the Past, bid us pause and ponder long upon the matchless Story of Versailles."

Online Resources

[Other books about French history by Charles River Editors](#)

[Other books about Versailles on Amazon](#)

Further Reading

Berger, Robert W. (1985a). *In the Garden of the Sun King: Studies on the Park of Versailles Under Louis XIV*. Washington, DC: Dumbarton Oaks Research Library.

Berger, Robert W. (1985b). *Versailles: The Château of Louis XIV*. University Park: The College Arts Association.

La Varende, Jean de (1959). *Versailles*. Paris: Henri Lefebvre.

Saule, Béatrix; Meyer, Daniel (2000). *Versailles Visitor's Guide*. Versailles: Éditions Art-Lys.

Free Books by Charles River Editors

We have brand new titles available for free most days of the week. To see which of our titles are currently free, click on this link.

Discounted Books by Charles River Editors

We have titles at a discount price of just 99 cents everyday. To see which of our titles are currently 99 cents, click on this link.

Printed in Great Britain
by Amazon